HOW
ARTIFICIAL INTELLIGENCE
WILL IMPACT SOCIETY

by Christa C. Hogan

ReferencePoint
Press®

San Diego, CA

TECHNOLOGY'S
IMPACT

For more information, contact:
ReferencePoint Press, Inc.
PO Box 27779
San Diego, CA 92198
www.ReferencePointPress.com

LIBRARY OF CONGRESS CATALOGING-IN-PUBLICATION DATA

Name: Hogan, Christa C., author.
Title: How Artificial Intelligence Will Impact Society / by Christa C. Hogan.
Description: San Diego, CA : ReferencePoint Press, Inc., [2019] | Series: Technology's Impact | Audience: Grades 9 to 12. | Includes bibliographical references and index.
Identifiers: LCCN 2018011543 (print) | LCCN 2018012677 (ebook) | ISBN 9781682824924 (ebook) | ISBN 9781682824917 (hardback)
Subjects: LCSH: Artificial intelligence—Social aspects—Juvenile literature. | Technological innovations—Social aspects—Juvenile literature. | CYAC: Artificial intelligence.
Classification: LCC Q335.4 (ebook) | LCC Q335.4 .H64 2018 (print) | DDC 006.3—dc23
LC record available at https://lccn.loc.gov/2018011543

Contents

IMPORTANT EVENTS IN THE DEVELOPMENT OF
ARTIFICIAL INTELLIGENCE

1958
McCarthy invents the programming language LISP, which is used in artificial intelligence applications.

1963
The AI Rancho Arm robot is used at Rancho Los Amigos Hospital in Downey, California.

1955
John McCarthy coins the term *artificial intelligence* (AI) at a research workshop on the topic.

1968
Marvin Minsky advises on the film *2001: A Space Odyssey*, featuring an AI computer named HAL 9000.

| 1950 | 1955 | 1960 | 1965 | 1970 |

1950
Alan Turing publishes "Computing Machinery and Intelligence," in which he proposes the Imitation Game.

1959
Arthur Samuel coins the term *machine learning*.

1970s
A period of time known as an AI winter begins due to disappointing research results, waning interest, and slashed funding.

2015
Bill Gates, Stephen Hawking, and Elon Musk warn of the dangers of unregulated AI research.

1981
AI winter begins to thaw; Digital Equipment Corporation's R1 system—also called XCON—configures orders and eventually saves the company $40 million a year.

2011
IBM's Watson beats the reigning champions of the US quiz show *Jeopardy!*

1980	1990	2000	2010	2015

2014
Creators of an AI chatbot called Eugene Goostman say it is the first AI program to pass the Turing Test.

1997
AI computer Deep Blue beats world chess champion Garry Kasparov.

1990
Rodney Brooks renews interest in the neural network method of programming AI.

2008
Apple iPhones include a voice-recognition app designed by Google.

Machines That Think

DeepFace may sound like a cool spy name. But it's actually Facebook's advanced facial recognition software. When Facebook suggests whom to tag in an image, DeepFace works behind the scenes. They're also witnessing a revolution in the use of artificial intelligence (AI) software.

DeepFace uses a type of AI called deep learning. Deep learning is a technique that teaches computers by example. It uses layers of **neural networks** to process data. DeepFace uses deep learning to find patterns or relationships between elements in the data. According to Facebook AI research scientist Yaniv Taigman, DeepFace learned to recognize images much as humans learn a task. Taigman said in a research paper he coauthored on DeepFace, "We trained it on the largest facial dataset to-date . . . four million facial images belonging to more than 4,000 identities."[1]

Once researchers gave DeepFace enough examples of matching images, the software program was able to recognize faces by itself. The more examples researchers provided for DeepFace, the better it performed its task. But how does DeepFace work?

BEHIND THE SCENES

First, DeepFace converts the image into a 3D model, which allows the software to view the face from different angles. For the most accuracy, the picture is adjusted to a forward-facing position. Next, DeepFace analyzes the image's facial features, such as brow shape and eye color. The software then searches for similarities in the facial features

Apple's iPhone X uses facial recognition in many ways. For example, it can analyze a user's facial expression and translate it into an animated character's expression.

of different images in its database. If the software recognizes enough similarities in several images, it concludes they must be of the same person. DeepFace then suggests friends to tag in a picture. It leaves the final decision up to the user.

DeepFace correctly identified people 97.25 percent of the time during tests. The average human given the same task succeeded 97.53 percent of the time. Creating software that performs as well as or better than humans is the goal of AI developers like Taigman. Taigman cofounded the Facebook AI Research (FAIR) group for this purpose. FAIR's goal is "to understand and develop systems with human-level intelligence."[2] AI developers argue that such software is not only achievable but also necessary. Rob Sherman, Facebook's Deputy Chief Privacy Officer, explains,

> *Like many tools, face recognition can be used for good purposes—like helping people securely unlock their mobile devices, log into their bank accounts and make digital payments. . . . It's even being used to find missing and kidnapped children and to help officials confirm whether travelers have authentic passports.[3]*

Humans can become overwhelmed by large amounts of data, such as the more than 350 million photographs uploaded to Facebook every day. However, AI software depends on it. Professor Xiaoou Tang of the Chinese University of Hong Kong, a leading expert on deep learning AI, explains that with AI, "The more data you have the more the accuracy and performance increases."[4]

DEFINING INTELLIGENCE

Facebook's facial recognition software is just one example of artificial intelligence. What exactly is AI? This simple question is actually quite difficult to answer, even for experts. The term *artificial* refers to something not occurring in nature. Intelligence, however, is a complex, human concept that's difficult to translate to machines. Neuroscientists, psychologists, and AI experts have all grappled with defining intelligence. They ask whether a machine that can play chess better than a human but can't balance a checkbook is intelligent.

Due to the complex questions surrounding intellect, the definition of AI is still in debate. However, AI is broadly considered to be a combination of software and hardware that can learn to perform tasks normally requiring human intelligence, such as problem solving and pattern recognition. For example, a robotic arm programmed to repeat a task on an assembly line is not AI. But a robotic arm that can learn a task and then adjust to a changing environment on its own is an example of AI.

AI TODAY

Modern AI systems use machine learning. Machine learning systems use **algorithms** to analyze data, learn from it, and make predictions. "Machine learning has really changed the game in the past three years," says Jeff Lawson, CEO of Twilio, a cloud communications platform. "It has leapfrogged the older generation of technology."[5]

WORDS IN CONTEXT

algorithms
Sets of rules to be followed in calculations performed by a computer.

With machine learning, programmers don't code specific tasks for AI machines. Instead they use large amounts of data to train the machine to predict an accurate outcome based on historical data. The shopping website Amazon uses machine learning to understand what products its customers are likely to purchase. Its software bases its decisions on customers' previous orders and searches. Experts caution that there are limitations to machine learning. The outcome depends on the quality of the data the machine is given, as well as the set of questions provided by programmers.

DeepFace can save people time if they want to tag many people in a group photo. But it has also raised privacy concerns.

AI TOMORROW

Today's AI can organize photo collections and help businesses better serve their customers. Researchers are now hard at work on the AI of tomorrow. Experts say robots with human-level reasoning are likely to remain science fiction for the time being. Still, the field of AI is growing rapidly.

Researchers predict the next generation of AI will benefit society in a number of ways. AI **exoskeletons** and robotic limbs are being developed to help make humans faster and stronger. They can also help people with disabilities.

AI home robots will help people prepare meals and remind them to take their medications. Experts also predict that AI machines will free up humans from dull tasks and provide more recreation time. Self-driving cars powered by AI will become an everyday reality that eliminates accidents.

AI AND SOCIETY

There are many advantages of AI technologies. Still, experts are concerned that the technology is advancing faster than it can be regulated. Corporations and governments could use AI technology to invade people's privacy. In 2017, Facebook was fined €150,000, at the time approximately $164,000, for "a massive compilation of personal data of internet users" that was put together without their knowledge.[6] Facebook was forced to delete all of the European facial recognition data it collected. DeepFace was made unavailable for European Facebook users as a result.

Use of AI technology can have serious consequences for privacy. It can also affect the world's economy and jobs market. Even as society enjoys the benefits of AI, experts seek to better understand AI's full impact on society.

How Does Artificial Intelligence Work?

AI is a complex and diverse field. It combines philosophical questions of human intellect and reason with cutting-edge math and science. Current AI theory and technology has also built upon the work of previous generations.

The field of AI didn't exist until the 1950s. However, people have been interested in learning machines for centuries. In the early 1600s, French philosopher and scientist René Descartes studied the connection between body and mind. He and other philosophers wanted to better understand human intellect and reasoning. Their work laid the foundation for current theories of human and machine intelligence.

In the 1800s, British mathematician George Boole created a system that turned complex human thoughts into simple equations. It was called Boolean logic. Boolean logic paved the way for the computer age.

By 1910, formal study of mathematics and logic gave Spanish inventor Leonardo Quevedo the tools to build a chess-playing machine. The machine used a mathematical algorithm to make decisions. A mechanical arm moved pieces. Quevedo proved that machines could do some things that scientists considered thought. Quevedo's chess machine was a precursor of modern AI game-playing machines.

The largest contributions to launching the field of AI came in the late 1930s and 1940s. Many inventions were spurred on by the need for code breakers during World War II. Engineers including Konrad Zuse, Tommy Flowers, and J. Presper Eckert Jr. created some of the first computers. Suddenly, equations that once took hours to solve could be calculated in a fraction of the time.

THE BIRTH OF MODERN AI

In 1950, British mathematician Alan Turing first asked whether machines could think. To answer that question, Turing developed a method to measure a machine's intelligence. Called the Imitation Game or the Turing Test, a human, called a judge, interacted with both another human and a computer in a **blind test**. The judge did not know which was the computer and which was the human. If the computer's responses were indistinguishable from a human being's, then Turing argued it could be said that the machine was thinking, or intelligent.

WORDS IN CONTEXT

blind test
A test in which elements of the experiment are unknown to the participant.

Critics of Turing's test suggest that it measures the machine's ability to mimic humans more than it demonstrates true intelligence. However, the Turing Test is still discussed in the field of AI today.

In 1955, American computer scientist John McCarthy coined the term *artificial intelligence*. The next year, McCarthy gathered a group of experts together for the Dartmouth Conference. Their goal was to explore the possibilities of AI.

McCarthy defined AI as "the science and engineering of making intelligent machines."[7] However, he admitted to the term's limitations from the beginning. "We cannot yet characterize in general what kinds

Alan Turing has been honored in some places with statues. The film The Imitation Game *is inspired by his life.*

of computational procedures we want to call intelligent," McCarthy said. "We understand some of the mechanisms of intelligence and not others."[8] McCarthy's contributions at the Dartmouth Conference and in future decades—including inventing the AI computing language LISP—have led many to call him the Father of AI.

Marvin Minsky was another important early AI pioneer. Minsky's 1960 paper, "Steps Toward Artificial Intelligence" became the roadmap for the next several decades of AI research. Minsky also invented the first electronic learning system. It used artificial neural networks modeled on the human brain. Minsky viewed neural networks, however, as too limited to accomplish human-level AI. His views led to a so-called AI winter, where researchers dismissed the potential of neural networks. AI researchers would revisit neural networks many years later, once more powerful technology became available.

The path to AI technology has had many twists and turns. Experts today are still debating whether machines can become truly intelligent or merely seem to be intelligent. To this end, discussions of AI are often divided into two categories—weak (or narrow) AI and strong (or general) AI.

WEAK OR NARROW AI

Weak (or narrow) AI uses machine learning to focus on solving a specific problem or performing a task. Weak AI may perform the task at a human or superhuman level. IBM's Deep Blue chess computer, which beat the world chess champion Gary Kasparov in 1997, is an example of weak AI. Weak AI cannot branch out to perform other tasks as humans can. Amazon's Alexa and Apple's Siri software use AI to process verbal commands, but they can only perform the narrow range of tasks they are programmed to do.

All AI today is considered to be weak or narrow. Not all weak AI is created equal, however. There are varying degrees of strength or aptitude within the category.

DEEP LEARNING AND ARTIFICIAL NEURAL NETWORKS

Some of the strongest narrow AI programs use the deep learning machine learning technique along with systems called artificial neural networks (ANNs). Deep learning is modeled on the human brain.

15

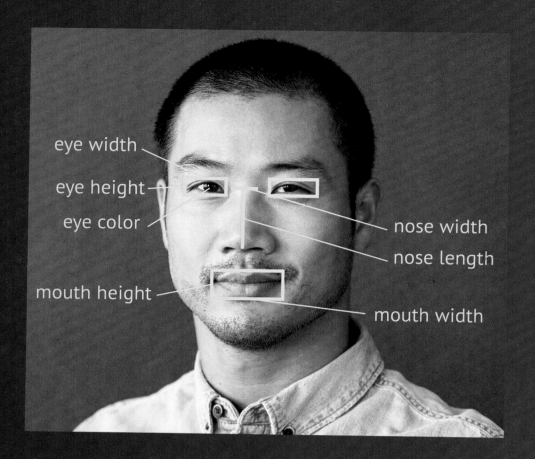

eye width
eye height
eye color
nose width
nose length
mouth height
mouth width

FACIAL RECOGNITION

AI designed for facial recognition is weak AI. It can only recognize a person by observing certain facial features. These features might include a person's eye color or length and width of nose. It could include mouth height and width. Without additional training, it cannot recognize or teach itself to learn to recognize people based on their voices. In addition, it is unable to do other things a human child could do, such as sing the alphabet or rhyme words. Weak AI is only good at a few tasks.

In a human brain, a system of connected **neurons** helps humans understand their world. In humans, the brain receives information through the senses. It then processes the information and generates a physical or emotional reaction. ANNs work in much the same way, although the scale is quite different.

Neural networks are limited by a lack of computational power in current technology. Today's networks have the equivalent of a few thousand to as many as 160 billion neural connections. In contrast, a human brain has 100 trillion connections. Deep learning adapts for this limitation by layering the networks. Each neural network is structured with an input layer, a number of middle layers, and an output layer. Information enters the input layer and processes through the network of neurons in the hidden layers. Information then passes on to the outer layer. The more connections in the hidden layers, the deeper the network and the more complex the results.

Deep learning has improved AI in tasks typically considered too difficult for machines. One such area is image and language recognition. Search-engine giant Google is a major advocate of deep learning AI technology. Google Assistant's speech recognition AI uses ANNs to better process spoken commands and questions. The system of algorithms used by deep learning software helps machines better understand spoken words as well as their intent. With Google Cloud Video Intelligence, deep learning AI analyzes videos for content and context, generating summaries. In each case, deep learning has helped Google's AI systems perform better and faster.

METHODS OF LEARNING

There are several ways AI systems can learn. Many AI systems use supervised learning. Supervised learning is a machine learning method that requires data to be labeled by humans. Developers use a training dataset as an example to teach the machine how to reach a desirable outcome. They then ask the machine to take what it learns

HOW TO TALK LIKE A HUMAN

Siri and her sometimes-humorous responses are a result of natural language processing (NLP) AI. NLP is the field of study in which computers learn how to talk like humans. This technology is present in a number of applications today, including smart refrigerators and assistants such as Siri.

Teaching machines to hold conversations with humans has long challenged AI developers. Even humans sometimes misunderstand what others are trying to say. Machines have an added disadvantage: They don't interact with the physical world like humans do. As a result, they often can't process concepts that humans take for granted.

Recent advancements in machine learning have made conversational technology possible. However, the technology still has a long way to go. Siri users are just as often frustrated as satisfied with her responses. Developers are working on methods of machine learning that will close the gap between machine language and natural language. Advancements in research and development will increase the ways we use conversational technology and improve user experience.

One way the technology could be used in the future is in more advanced personal assistants. AI assistants could respond to voice commands and perform a variety of tasks. Researchers could use an AI assistant to analyze thousands of studies and generate a new hypothesis. Senior citizens could ask a robotic helper to bring them a glass of water. In the future, conversational assistants could be embedded in everything from operating room tables to household appliances to clothing.

and apply that knowledge to a whole new set of data. Supervised learning models have helped financial institutions predict how likely a customer is to default on a loan.

Another method of AI training is called reinforcement learning. With reinforcement learning, an AI system learns from trial and error. The system is rewarded for making the right decisions, much as a rat is rewarded with a bit of cheese for finding its way through a maze. The rewards strengthen the system's connection to the desired outcomes. Experts have found that reinforcement learning works well in a set environment such as on a chessboard or a highway. However, this method requires large amounts of data and simulation. Machines using reinforcement learning struggle to adapt to an unpredictable, real-world environment.

A third method for training AI is called unsupervised learning. This method uses unlabeled data and asks a machine to predict an outcome using more complex algorithms. The machine's algorithms are capable of making order out of unstructured data. For instance, when given a collection of unlabeled images, the machine is able to sort animals from humans. The machine may further group the animals in four- or two-legged varieties and the humans into male and female, all without any human supervision. Unsupervised learning reduces a machine's reliance on humans.

AI developers use all three types of machine learning to develop robust software. However, experts including Facebook's director of AI research, Yann LeCun, believe that unsupervised learning will unlock more advanced AI. LeCun says:

> The challenge of the next several years, is to let machines learn from raw, unlabeled data, such as video or text. This is known as unsupervised learning. AI systems today do not possess

*'**common sense**,' which humans . . . acquire by observing the world and acting in it. . . . Some of us see unsupervised learning as the key towards machines with common sense.*[9]

ALPHAGO: WEAK AI

Google also acquired the AI company DeepMind in 2014. DeepMind is currently developing AI to aid in health and technology advancements. The company is perhaps best known, however, for developing AlphaGo.

AlphaGo was the first computer program to defeat a professional human Go player, South Korean champion Lee Sedol. An ancient Chinese board game, Go is considered to be one of the most complex games for a machine due to the amount of human **intuition** needed to win. According to DeepMind, although AlphaGo is weak AI, it is able to perform at a superhuman level. DeepMind observed that "during the games, AlphaGo played a handful of highly inventive winning moves, several of which . . . were so surprising they overturned hundreds of years of received wisdom."[10]

The next version, AlphaGo Zero, surpassed its predecessor. Previous versions of AlphaGo learned to play by processing thousands of human games, a type of reinforcement learning. This time, AlphaGo Zero played millions of games only against itself, beginning with random moves. The system never received any human supervision. It learned, as the youngest of human minds do, from

Sedol, right, won just one out of five games against AlphaGo. An AlphaGo programmer made moves for the machine.

its own mistakes and achievements. Unlike AlphaGo, AlphaGo Zero wasn't limited by the constraints of human abilities or knowledge.

AlphaGo's results are impressive, says AI expert Pedro Domingos of the University of Washington. However, systems like AlphaGo don't mean society is on the verge of achieving truly intelligent machines. In order to achieve its success, Domingos points out, the system still has to play millions more games than a human does to become a Go champion. "What would be really impressive would be if AlphaGo beat

Lee Sedol after playing roughly as many games as he played in his career before becoming a champion. We're nowhere near that."[11]

STRONG OR GENERAL AI

Today's weak AI is agile and effective, but it is also very narrow. Deep Blue plays an excellent game of chess. AlphaGo can beat any human at Go. However, neither can play a simple child's game of tic-tac-toe. They aren't programmed for it.

To imagine the difference between weak/narrow AI and strong/general AI, consider the AlphaGo program. Now, imagine a version that also does everything else the human mind is capable of doing. Some AI experts hope that the AI of the future will be truly strong AI that demonstrates a broad intelligence.

Strong AI, also known as Artificial General Intelligence (AGI), will show true human intelligence. An AGI machine will be able to observe the world—sights, smells, and sounds—and use that data to solve a variety of problems. "General intelligence is what people do," explains David Hanson, CEO of Hanson Robotics. "The most powerful concept of general intelligence is that it's adaptive."[12] It can hold a conversation, make purchases at the store, and apply a learned skill to new situations.

OBSTACLES TO AGI

AGI can only be found in fiction today. Many researchers are working to create AGI. But the current understanding of AI presents several obstacles to this goal.

For example, AI machines are very good at some tasks considered difficult for humans, such as chess. Tasks that are simple for humans, such as recognizing faces and voices, are more

KILLER ROBOTS: FUTURE FACT OR MOVIE FICTION?

Movies featuring AI often exploit society's fear of smart machines to dramatic ends. In the 2004 movie *I, Robot*, an AI system enlists hordes of robots to subdue humanity. The coldly menacing AI system HAL 9000 kills the crew of a space ship in *2001: A Space Odyssey*. Movies with such alarming premises prompt questions. Should society be concerned about AI going awry, or is it all Hollywood hype?

Some AI experts say that depictions of Terminator-like robots are inaccurate and far-fetched. Renowned AI researcher Stuart Russell, however, believes Hollywood doesn't go far enough. "There's not nearly enough work on making sure [AI] isn't a threat," says Russell, who advocates for a ban on weapons that can work without human aid.

Russell created his own short film, "Slaughterbots," to help influence a United Nations (UN) decision on a ban in late 2017. The film portrays a disturbing near-future scenario. Intelligent, weaponized drones use facial-recognition AI in targeted attacks on civilians and politicians. The UN didn't reach any conclusions on a ban in 2017. However, Russell's film received 2 million views and attracted media attention.

Many AI experts share Russell's concerns. However, they argue that sensationalizing the subject in movies distracts from the real work being done in AI. "[AI] is going to alleviate poverty. It's going to cure diseases," says Robert Atkinson, president of the Information Technology and Innovation Foundation. "We should be tripling AI research. But when we talk about it in these apocalyptic terms, we're going in the exact opposite direction."

Graham Vyse, "Should We Fear 'Terminator'-Style Robot Uprisings? A Washington Think Tank Discusses," *Inside Sources*, June 30, 2015. www.insidesources.com

difficult. As computer scientist Donald Knuth puts it, "AI has by now succeeded in doing essentially everything that requires 'thinking' but has failed to do most of what people and animals do 'without thinking'—that, somehow, is much harder!"[13] For instance, modern AI still lacks innate human traits such as common sense. Common sense

Computers have made many technological advances. However, even the biggest supercomputer is incapable of powering AGI.

underpins much of human understanding. Humans develop common sense by interacting with their world in ways that machines cannot.

"The lack of common sense reasoning is a major obstacle," admits Ernest Davis, a computer scientist with New York University who studies common sense and machines. "There's large amounts of basic understanding of the world that we haven't been able to get programs to do. . . . But we don't know how we ourselves understand the world, mostly, so these traits are incredibly difficult to **emulate** in a program."[14]

Another limitation AI developers face in creating AGI is a lack of computing power. Today's successful machine learning and deep learning AI require massive amounts of calculations just to reach the level of weak AI. Technological advances have made these calculations possible. Experts say that AGI will require another jump in technology before it can be fully developed. For example, in 2014, German and Japanese researchers used the fourth-most powerful computer in the world to simulate human brain activity. The computer took 40 minutes to simulate one second of brain activity.

No one machine is yet capable of walking, talking, and performing as a human. Instead, a variety of weak AI systems are used to accomplish each narrow task. From DeepFace's facial recognition software to driverless vehicles, weak AI is the only game in town for now. In the meantime, researchers are focusing on making today's machines smarter.

How Does AI Impact Society?

Artificial intelligence is already used in a number of everyday technologies. AI pioneer Andrew Ng believes that AI empowers society. "Just as electricity transformed many industries roughly 100 years ago," Ng says, "AI will also now change nearly every major industry—healthcare, transportation, entertainment, manufacturing—enriching the lives of countless people. I am more excited than ever about where AI can take us."[15]

Ng believes that artificial intelligence will take over boring tasks. Technologies such as **autonomous** cars will replace human drivers just as machines have replaced humans in many physically repetitive manufacturing jobs. Other AI experts are less optimistic. Perhaps most notably, Tesla founder and CEO Elon Musk called for government regulation of the AI industry. Musk believes that smart machines in the wrong hands pose a greater threat to humanity than nuclear weapons. Doomsday scenarios aside, a 2017 study titled "Workforce of the Future" also found that automation and AI could affect 38 percent of American jobs by the early 2030s. Regardless of one's view, AI has a huge impact across society.

MANUFACTURING

Ng is working on using AI to improve factories and manufacturing with his business, Landing.AI. The company creates technologies and systems that help remove repetitive tasks from manufacturing jobs. "It is now time to build not just an AI-powered IT industry, but an AI-powered society," says Ng. "One in which our physical needs, health care, transportation, food, and lodging are more accessible through AI, and where every person is freed from repetitive mental drudgery."[16]

Ng is developing an AI camera that uses deep learning technology to find defects in manufactured items. Humans currently do this repetitive job. The AI requires only five examples to train the system. This allows the system to be more adaptable so workers can retrain it on multiple tasks. Ng is quick to admit that his AI robots could take jobs from manufacturing workers. His firm is working to find ways to retrain employees to take on higher-skill positions.

> **WORDS IN CONTEXT**
>
> **autonomous**
> Having to do with an object that acts independently of outside forces.

The manufacturing industry has long been replacing humans with robot workers. At times the robots have become dangerous. The first person known to have been killed by a robot was Robert Williams in 1979. Williams worked in a Ford automotive plant in Michigan. The robot malfunctioned, and Williams climbed into the robot's area to help. The robot began working again, killing Williams.

Robotic accidents are tragic. But AI experts point out that they make up a very small number of work-related deaths. Since 1984, robots in the workplace have killed approximately thirty people. By comparison, there were 5,190 fatal work injuries reported in 2016 alone. Experts say that machines have actually helped lower the overall accident rates in manufacturing. The inclusion of AI software in robots further improves human safety. AI can help make a machine aware that a person is present, preventing the machine from injuring that person.

AI can also make manufacturing more efficient and less costly. Smart machines can quickly troubleshoot problems that arise during manufacturing without slowing down or stopping production. This saves companies time and money. The result is more affordable products for consumers, helping companies stay competitive.

TRANSPORTATION

AI is also advancing quickly in the field of transportation, especially with autonomous vehicles. In early 2017, Google-owned Waymo offered a driverless taxi service in a small neighborhood of Phoenix, Arizona. Minivans were equipped with AI software as well as cameras, a radar system, and sensors. The AI software and hardware worked in tandem to help the vehicle safely navigate traffic.

To hail a Waymo taxi, travelers used an app. Once inside the taxi, passengers could push an emergency "Pull Over" button if needed. The taxis began operating with a Waymo employee sitting in the driver's seat to reassure new passengers. By the end of the year, however, the driver's seat was empty.

The National Highway Traffic Safety Administration developed a leveled system to differentiate the types of automated vehicles that operate without human aid. An ordinary car with no autonomous features is Level 0. A fully autonomous car is Level 5. Waymo's taxis are considered to be Level 4 autonomous vehicles. Level 4 vehicles are highly autonomous. They can navigate a confined area with little driver interference. In comparison, Level 5 vehicles would be able to take a passenger to any destination under any weather conditions. In October 2017, American technology company NVIDIA released Drive PX Pegasus. Pegasus is an AI computer that can operate fully autonomous Level 5 robotaxis. NVIDIA founder and CEO Jensen Huang said, "Creating a fully self-driving car is one of society's most

Waymo is working to create fully autonomous self-driving cars. In early 2018, they were testing their technology in twenty-five cities in the United States.

important endeavors—and one of the most challenging to deliver. The breakthrough AI computing performance and efficiency of Pegasus is crucial for the industry to realize this vision."[17]

Pegasus robotaxis will eventually be able to take passengers anywhere they want to go. Trunk space will be limited, however. The NVIDIA AI chip performs more than 320 trillion operations per second. That much computing takes plenty of hardware.

Pegasus robotaxi trunks will likely resemble **data centers** with stacks of computers. Regardless, twenty-five automotive partners were developing Pegasus robotaxis in 2017. Huang predicts that fully automated AI robotaxis will be available in the near future.

BENEFITS OF AI IN TRANSPORTATION

AI experts point to three benefits to society of autonomous, AI-equipped vehicles. Experts believe that autonomous vehicles will save lives. In 2016, traffic fatalities in the United States rose to the highest rate in nearly a decade. According to the National Safety Council, 40,200 people died as a result of traffic accidents. Human error was blamed for 90 percent of the accidents where fatalities occurred. According to the Centers for Disease Control and Prevention (CDC), 1.25 million people are killed on roadways around the world each year. The CDC also states that, "Road traffic injuries are estimated to be the eighth leading cause of death globally and the leading cause of death for young people aged 15 to 29."[18]

Experts estimate that self-driving cars equipped with AI chips can reduce traffic fatalities by as much as 90 percent. But the gradual introduction of autonomous vehicles to modern roadways hasn't been without incident. Society often debates whether AI can be trusted to make life-or-death decisions. And some people don't realize the technology's current limits.

Automaker Tesla makes the Model S, one of the most popular electric cars available today. The Model S includes a feature called Autopilot, which assists drivers. It can make adjustments to the speed of the car based on the speed of traffic around the car, keep the car in a lane, or change lanes. But it cannot drive autonomously. In May 2016, Joshua Brown's Tesla Model S crashed into a semitruck while on Autopilot. The vehicle was traveling at 74 miles per hour (119 km/h), 9 miles per hour (14 km/h), nine miles over the speed limit. Brown was killed. The truck's driver wasn't injured. Later evaluation found that the Tesla's Autopilot, which Elon Musk calls an "assist feature" that's not fully autonomous, performed as programmed.[19] However, during a 41-minute drive, Brown's hands were on the steering wheel for a total of only 25 seconds. Autopilot warned Brown seven times within the previous 40 minutes to keep his hands on the steering wheel. Tesla believes the accident occurred because the Autopilot couldn't distinguish between the semitruck's broad, white side and the sky. The driver, however, had a clear view. He may have been able to avoid the crash if he were more alert. Despite the unfortunate fatality, AI experts believe fully autonomous vehicles will make the roadways safer. For example, the number of crashes involving a Tesla fell 40 percent after the company introduced the Autopilot's Autosteer feature in 2016.

Using autonomous vehicles and lowering the rate of accidents also lowers the cost to society. The World Health Organization (WHO) estimates that road traffic crashes cost most countries 3 percent of their gross domestic product. WHO research shows that traffic fatalities disproportionately affect low- and middle-income communities. Researchers suggest factors including poor infrastructure, a lack of road signs in poor neighborhoods, and an increase in bicycles and pedestrians play a role. Low-income drivers also tend to drive older cars with fewer safety features. The use of autonomous vehicles could help protect the most vulnerable communities in society.

Autonomous vehicles could also provide society with an increase in leisure time. In 2013, the US Census Bureau found that "86 percent of all workers commuted to work by private vehicle, either driving alone or carpooling."[20] The average commute for US workers is twenty-six minutes, or more than five hundred days over a lifetime. With the availability of fully autonomous vehicles, American workers could use their commuting time for something other than driving. They could read a book or catch up on much-needed sleep.

HEALTH CARE

In recent years, hospitals and physicians have digitized patient records. This has created a large body of data suitable for AI technologies such as IBM's Watson. Watson's ability to recognize patterns in large data sets is proving especially useful in health care.

In 2015, IBM partnered with cancer treatment centers, including the University of North Carolina's Lineberger Center. IBM wanted to see if its Watson for Genomics software could help doctors working with cancer patients tailor-fit treatments to their patients. Each year, 1.6 million Americans are diagnosed with cancer. Some of these patients don't respond to traditional treatments. Oncologists have turned to genetic sequencing to target their patients' specific cancer-causing genetic mutations. The sequencing for a single patient's **genome**, however, produces more than one hundred gigabytes of data. In addition, oncologists have to process their patients' medical records as well as the latest medical studies and research. Deciphering this avalanche of data can be a slow process that costs precious time.

WORDS IN CONTEXT

genome
An organism's complete DNA, including its genes.

WHAT IS WATSON?

Ken Jennings and Brad Rutter were the reigning champions of the TV quiz show *Jeopardy!* in 2011. Together, they had earned $5 million. But they were about to get a run for their money. Their new competition, Watson, was a room-sized question-answering computer. For years, engineers struggled to create AI machines that adequately processed natural language such as that used in *Jeopardy!* questions. Now Watson, named for IBM's founder, used artificial intelligence techniques to help untangle questions and hunt down answers. IBM engineers hoped that Watson would be a new breakthrough in AI.

In the *Jeopardy!* studio, Jennings and Rutter stood on either side of Watson, which was represented onstage by a glowing flat screen. Watson could not connect to the internet. Instead, Watson stored 200 million pages of information from a variety of sources, including the entire contents of Wikipedia. IBM used the data and deep learning techniques to train Watson. By the big day, Watson's data, training, and 2,208 computer processors were ready to answer questions.

Over three matches, Watson's winnings totaled $77,147 compared to Jennings's $24,000 and Rutter's $21,600. Watson's technology made important advancements in language processing AI. Watson could better analyze the context of human language in massive amounts of data and answer questions in terms that users could understand.

IBM brought Watson to *Jeopardy!* to help show off their technology, but now Watson is used for other purposes. Watson helps oncologists treat cancer patients, financial advisers manage risks, and lawyers sort through case histories.

Watson was given the information of 1,018 former cancer patients to analyze. Each case normally took weeks to review. However, the program completed the reviews in only a few minutes each. Watson created an accessible report with recommendations on drugs that corresponded with the patient's genetic sequencing. The Lineberger Center's molecular tumor board of physicians then reviewed the program's results. Of the 1,018 cases, the board identified 703 cases that would qualify for genetic sequencing. Watson confirmed those cases and also identified new **therapeutic** options based on the latest research for an additional 323 patients.

The Lineberger Center's William Kim said, "I'm optimistic that as we get more sequencing data, well-annotated treatment information, as well as therapy response, tools like Watson for Genomics will begin to show their true promise." Kim explained that Watson helps patients feel they are receiving the best treatment: "It's very reassuring for patients to know that we're able to explore all possible options for them in a very systematic manner."[21]

AI software has the potential to save time and improve patient care. When paired with robotics, AI could also produce better results for patients. The Smart Tissue Autonomous Robot (STAR) is used for complex soft tissue surgeries. Researchers train STAR using the best surgeons' techniques. Then, during surgery, STAR's vision system uses special tags as a guide. The tags are placed on soft tissue that's likely to shift during surgery. One camera tracks the tags, while a 3D camera records images of the surgical site. All of this information is converted into data, which allows STAR to plan the surgery. STAR then modifies its plan to adjust to shifting soft tissue during the operation. Initial surgeries have shown that STAR's stitches are more consistent and leak-resistant than an experienced surgeon's. Human surgeons are still involved during the procedure, placing the tags. Researchers believe, however, that STAR is one step closer to having fully autonomous surgeons in the operating room.

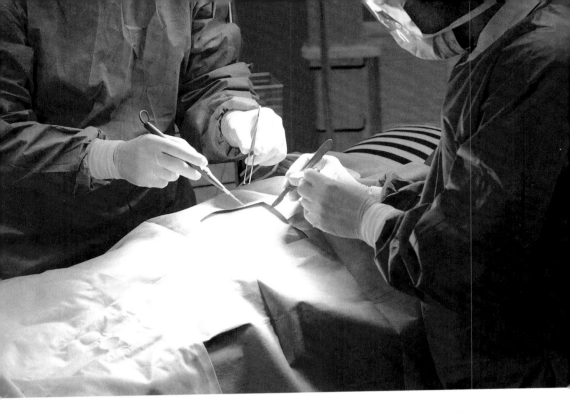

While surgeons are highly skilled, human hands are not always as precise as they need to be. AI robots could work with a precision that humans do not have.

Axel Krieger coauthored a study of STAR's performance and is optimistic about the technology. He says:

> *I believe this will come about first for small sub-functions of surgery and get more and more complex, similarly to autonomous cars, where small features such as brake-assist slowly morphed into more and more autonomy. I absolutely would trust a robot like that for my surgery, once it is fully developed and validated.*[22]

In the future, a suite of AI assistants might work with physicians and surgeons. IBM's Watson could serve as a surgical assistant, answering surgeons' spoken questions. Robots like STAR could act as the surgeon's hands, eliminating natural hand tremors. Machine learning algorithms could help physicians find patterns among patient symptoms to diagnose and treat diseases earlier. Surgical students could learn by watching game-playing AI similar to AlphaGo simulate the same problem over and over.

Using robotics during surgery comes with risks, however. Cornell University studied robotic surgeries taking place from 2000 to 2013. Of the nearly 2 million surgeries, 144 deaths and 1,391 injuries were linked to robotic accidents. The most common incidents reported included device and system errors and malfunctions. Overall, however, researchers concluded that "adoption of advanced techniques in design and operation of robotic surgical systems . . . may reduce these preventable incidents in the future."[23]

ROBOTS WITH EMOTIONS

Researchers predict that by 2060 there will be more than 98 million people over the age of sixty-five in the United States alone. This will create a significant load on the country's health-care systems. So companies today are developing a variety of AI robots to help seniors. Paro is a therapeutic AI robot that resembles a white baby seal. Paro is currently used in hospitals and nursing homes across Europe and Japan. The adorable robot uses five different sensors, including hearing and touch sensors, to detect its environment. Paro interacts with patients based on the information gathered from its sensors. The robot acts like a real therapeutic animal. It has been shown to reduce patients' stress and motivate them to socialize more with others.

Another robot that engages human emotions is Pepper. Pepper is almost 4 feet (1.2 m) tall. It has a head, arms, and a tablet mounted on its chest. It gets around on a three-wheeled base that allows it to make sharp turns. Pepper is an "emotional robot" according to its creators at SoftBank Robotics. "Pleasant and likeable," the company says of its creation, "Pepper is much more than a robot, he

When researchers studied dog, cat, and seal robots, they found people were disappointed with the dog and cat because they compared the robots to the real animals. Most people have not interacted with a seal, so developers made the therapeutic robot Paro a seal.

is a genuine **humanoid** companion created to communicate with you in the most natural and intuitive way."[24] Pepper recognizes faces and emotions and adjusts its behavior to its owner's moods. It responds appropriately by changing its expression or the color of its eyes. It also displays messages and images on its tablet. Pepper is currently being used in Japanese homes and to interact with customers in businesses. Robots like Pepper could one day be used to help isolated or homebound persons.

ADDITIONAL AI BENEFITS

AI can do a lot to improve people's lives. The technology is being used in many innovative ways in health care, business, and disaster relief. In 2011, AI robots helped shut down the Fukushima nuclear reactors in Japan. The reactors were overwhelmed by an earthquake and tsunami. Engineers were uncertain how much radiation was leaking

AI SUPER SOLDIERS

The army medic hefts a wounded man onto his shoulder. The AI exoskeleton bracing the medic's legs recognizes the added weight and makes an adjustment. The medic is then easily able to lift the soldier. The medic carries the soldier up five flights of stairs to safety.

Bionic exoskeletons are one way that the US military is using artificial intelligence. Developed by Lockheed Martin, the FORTIS exoskeleton uses motors, a lightweight frame, and a lithium ion battery. The exoskeleton belts around the soldier's waist and connects to each hip and leg. Sensors along the frame tell FORTIS's AI software where the soldier is and how quickly he or she is moving. The exoskeleton then adjusts the soldier's gait to relieve stress on the soldier's knees. FORTIS also helps soldiers run faster, carry heavier loads, and exert less energy.

The US Navy tested a version of FORTIS that included an arm to help support heavy tools. Ship maintenance requires crew members to heft riveters and sandblasters in addition to loading heavy supplies. Naval researchers found that half of all work time was nonproductive due to the breaks required to recover from heavy labor. Lockheed says that FORTIS reduced sailors' fatigue by 300 percent and improved productivity by 200 to 2,700 percent. AI exoskeletons could be used in any industry that requires humans to repeatedly lift and carry heavy objects.

inside the power plant. The situation was considered too dangerous for humans. So the robotics company iRobot sent six AI robots to help shut down the reactors.

The AI robots entered the plant and relayed information back through video cameras. Engineers then read pressure gauges, determined which pipes were damaged, and measured radiation levels. Rodney Brooks, cofounder of iRobot, said of the machines:

> The robots we sent to Fukushima were not just remote control machines. They had an Artificial Intelligence (AI) based operating system, known as Aware 2.0, that allowed the robots to build maps, plan optimal paths, right themselves should they tumble down a slope, and to retrace their path when they lost contact with their human operators.[25]

The robots were instrumental in helping the engineers safely shut down the plant and prevent any deaths. Later, robots were also used to vacuum debris, climb piles of rubble, and cut through fences. Additional robots are being developed to clean up similar events in the future. AI powers these robots' decision making, helping the robots work together with human operators. The Fukushima plant shutdown is an important demonstration of the benefits that AI brings to society. AI can be used to protect humans during catastrophic events such as this.

Can We Trust AI?

Weak AI presents several challenges for designers and users. One of those challenges is algorithmic bias. Bias is an unfair preference for or discrimination against certain characteristics or people groups. How could a machine be biased? And what impact could algorithmic bias have on society?

At its simplest, weak AI is a set of algorithms trained by developers on large data sets to perform a task. Bias could enter the system at a number of points. First, the data used in deep learning could contain **disparities** that teach bias and prejudice to the system. An AI system could quickly learn from humanity's worst impulses. For example, in 2016, Microsoft released an AI Twitter **chatbot** named Tay. Tay was designed to respond to its followers in an entertaining way that reflected its audience. The more it spoke with users, the more it learned to personalize its conversations. Within hours Tay was repeating hate speech and promoting neo-Nazi views. Tay was taken offline. One of the best ways to prevent this kind of bias in AI, experts say, is to avoid training AI systems on biased information.

Second, there's a lack of diversity among the developers who create the systems. Most AI developers today are male, fairly wealthy, and educated. Women, Hispanics, and African Americans are underrepresented in the field.

Experts say this lack of diversity has resulted in a "like me" bias in many programs, where systems reflect their developers. For example, research shows that some facial analysis algorithms built in Asia by Asian developers tend to perform better with Asian faces than with white ones. On the other hand, programs developed in mostly Caucasian countries often read Asian faces as having their eyes closed and struggle to recognize black faces.

AI is used increasingly to make decisions once made by humans. For instance, bankers determine whether or not to offer loans based on AI software. Facial-recognition scanners bar or admit travelers at airports. As a result, algorithmic bias has a broad impact on society.

In 2016, the nonprofit group ProPublica conducted an investigation into an AI program used by US courts for risk-assessment. Correctional Offender Management Profiling for Alternative Sanctions (COMPAS) is being used in hundreds of courts across the United States. The system analyzes defendants' history and determines how likely they are to commit another crime within two years. Judges then use the information provided by COMPAS in determining sentences, setting bails, and deciding probations.

ProPublica studied the risk scores of 7,000 people arrested in Broward County, Florida, from 2013 to 2014. It then checked in with defendants two years later to determine the accuracy of COMPAS's predictions. In forecasting violent crime, COMPAS was correct only 20 percent of the time. Of those designated as likely to re-offend, only 61 percent were arrested for any subsequent crimes within two years. ProPublica also found that COMPAS's algorithms falsely flagged black defendants as future criminals twice as often as white defendants.

LABELED FACES IN THE WILD

Labeled Faces in the Wild (LFW) is a popular collection of 13,000 facial images of more than 5,700 celebrities. Developers created the collection for the purpose of improving facial recognition programs. The images were pulled from the Web. Faces are presented in a variety of lighting conditions and poses. Companies such as Google and Facebook have used LFW in developing and training their AI facial recognition software programs.

Since LFW was released in 2007, AI software has continued to improve at facial recognition. In 2014, a Chinese research team used LFW to create a program with 98.52 percent accuracy—even higher than human ability. Facial recognition software is now being used across the globe to improve security, detect fraud, and organize data.

However, experts say that LFW isn't representative of the general population. A 2014 study of LFW found that 83 percent of the images were of white people. Seventy-eight percent of the images were of men. This discrepancy may contribute to a bias in facial recognition programs developed using LFW.

Joy Buolamwini of the Algorithmic Justice League, an organization that aims to get rid of bias in algorithms, says that facial recognition software often does not recognize African American faces such as hers. Buolamwini says the problem stems from algorithmic bias in programs that rely on flawed databases like LFW. The solution, she suggests, is to create data sets that better reflect the full spectrum of human faces.

Black defendants were 77 percent more likely to be shown as being at higher risk of committing a future violent crime. They were also 45 percent more likely to be predicted to commit a future crime. COMPAS is one of the most widely used criminal ranking systems in the country. Judges have cited the program's scores as part of the information used in determining sentencing.

Northpointe, the for-profit company that created COMPAS, disputed the investigation's findings. ProPublica points out that one of the difficulties in understanding algorithmic bias is lack of information on how AI comes to its conclusions. "The company does not publicly disclose the calculations used to arrive at defendants' risk scores, so it is not possible for either defendants or the public to see what might be driving the disparity," ProPublica says.[26] More transparency of AI systems is needed to better understand algorithmic bias. But in general, AI experts say that a more diverse workforce would help guard against this kind of bias.

Society often views AI as an impartial decision-maker. As a result, we trust AI to make even minor decisions for us—from what music we hear to which news stories we see. Unfortunately, AI can also be a reflection of our worst prejudices. For AI to be part of creating a more equitable future, society will need to be honest about its own shortcomings.

AI AND PRIVACY

The success of technologies such as facial recognition software has led to a global explosion in its use. Many organizations now use AI to interpret video and still images to prevent crime. The state of Delaware plans to use smart dashboard cameras to detect the presence of fugitives or victims in a vehicle. An Israeli company uses AI to analyze security video footage to identify targets quickly. In Russia, businesses are using facial recognition software to single out problem customers and potential shoplifters. While these uses of AI are helpful, experts warn that they could come at the cost of personal privacy.

In 2017, two Stanford University researchers developed AI facial recognition software that guessed a person's sexual orientation. The study's program used neural networks to examine the facial features of 35,326 images. Researchers trained the facial recognition software on which characteristics experts believe may be linked to sexual orientation, such as certain expressions and grooming styles. Using these traits as a guideline, the program distinguished accurately between gay and heterosexual men 81 percent of the time, compared to a human observer at 61 percent. When the number of images of a person was increased from one to five, the program's accuracy leapt to 91 percent.

The authors of this controversial study weren't interested in uncovering someone's sexual orientation. Instead, they hoped the study would highlight some of the dangers of using AI technology. "Given that companies and governments are increasingly using computer vision algorithms to detect people's intimate traits, our findings expose a threat to the privacy and safety of gay men and women."[27] The authors pointed out that homosexuality is still illegal in some countries, and that there were reports of governments intending to use facial recognition software to predict criminal intent. The researchers hoped their study would raise awareness about the ethical concerns of using AI in such a manner.

CYBERCRIME

When it comes to AI and cybercrime, there's good news and bad news. "We have AI, but so do the bad guys," says Ann Johnson, Microsoft's Vice President of Enterprise and Cybersecurity. And the bad guys aren't going away any time soon. "It is a multi-trillion-dollar industry . . . and they are working together in ways they never did before."[28]

One common criminal method is to use AI in phishing schemes. Criminals use AI software to email or post links that lead users to download **malware** or ask for personal information such as passwords or credit card numbers. Criminals often use these techniques to steal important information they can then use or resell.

Two developers at security company ZeroFox wanted to better understand just how well AI works for phishing schemes. They created an AI tool called Social Network Automated Phishing and Reconnaissance (SNAP_R). The tool used neural networks to analyze more than two million Twitter posts. SNAP_R then posted phishing links on Twitter that would appeal to users based on that data. The tool's posts sounded surprisingly human.

Researchers pitted SNAP_R against a human journalist. Over a two-hour period they went head-to-head, posting phishing messages on Twitter. They then compared the success rates of the two methods. SNAP_R tweeted 6.75 tweets per minute. Of the 819 users sent phishing messages by AI, 275 victims took the bait. Meanwhile, the journalist tweeted only 1.075 tweets a minute. Only 49 users out of 226 actually clicked through on the harmless links. The ZeroFox developers attributed SNAP_R's success to the unique risks associated with social media and AI's ability to quickly target vulnerable users with a highly personalized message.

At the same time, AI is being used to fight back against spammers. One example is the re:Scam chatbot created in 2017 by Netsafe, a cybersecurity nonprofit. Scam emails often falsely promise large cash winnings in exchange for users' personal information. Netsafe invites users to forward scam emails to a company email account. The security company then unleashes the re:Scam chatbot on the scammers. The chatbot holds convincingly human email conversations with the scammers requesting more information. The scammers, unaware that they are speaking with a chatbot and not a human victim, take the bait. Re:Scam wastes the scammers' time, which damages their profits and holds them up from moving on to more unsuspecting targets. Meanwhile, re:Scam also helps Netsafe analyze important information used to fight future scammers. Netsafe estimated that by April 2018 the chatbot wasted more than five years of scammers' time.

HACKING PROBLEMS

Though chatbots designed to thwart scammers might seem amusing, AI crimes are serious. Experts are concerned that hackers could take advantage of weaknesses in AI systems, such as those used in driverless cars. In 2016, a group of hackers took remote control of a Tesla Model S to demonstrate the security weakness of autonomous vehicles. From 12 miles (19 km) away, the hackers were able to interfere with the car's electronic features, including the brakes and door locks. When Tesla learned of the breach, the company quickly issued a software update to its vehicles. However, the incident served as an example of the potential threat to autonomous vehicles connected to the internet.

Sarah Abboud, a spokesperson for ride and delivery service Uber, said security is a top priority as the company moves forward with using driverless vehicles. "Our team of security experts are constantly exploring new defenses for the future of autonomous vehicles, including data integrity and abuse detection."[29] Yet as AI technologies advance, so will the capabilities of cyber criminals. AI developers are constantly analyzing their systems' weaknesses and developing better security against breaches.

Facial recognition software, cybercrime, and inadequate technology are just a few examples of how AI can threaten privacy. Experts say much more research is needed to fully address

AI FIGHT CLUB

AI's neural networks excel at recognizing patterns and changes in those patterns. This means the technology is especially useful at detecting cybersecurity threats and defending against cyberattacks. But training AI to avoid being duped can be a challenge. To that end, a number of AI fight clubs, in which two AI systems attack each other, help developers create systems that can defend against sophisticated attacks.

Google's AI research machine Google Brain and data science platform Kaggle created the Competition on Adversarial Attacks and Defenses. The contest pitted two AI systems against one another in three challenges. First, the attacker tried to confuse the other system into functioning incorrectly, a move called a non-targeted adversarial attack. The second battle attempt was a targeted adversarial attack. Here, the attacker attempted to get the other AI to incorrectly classify data. Third, the AI had to defend against attacks by developing its own smart defense system. The event organizers planned to use the information gained from the competition to locate and fix vulnerabilities in AI systems.

Capture the Flag (CTF) contests are another example of AI fight clubs. Teams compete to solve security problems or capture and defend a system. The Defense Advanced Research Projects Agency, part of the US Department of Defense, developed the first fully autonomous CTF competition in 2016. In the Cyber Grand Challenge (CGC) seven systems competed autonomously for 12 hours. Scores were based on protecting their hosts, locating vulnerabilities, and functioning properly. Events such as CGC help AI developers identity weaknesses and better train AI systems to defend against an active adversary without human supervision.

the concern. One thing is clear: If AI is to be trusted, its creators need to be cautious in how it's developed and used.

CAN AI SAFELY DRIVE CARS?

One large danger of AI, especially in technology like self-driving cars, is the lack of common sense. Self-driving cars cannot drive through construction zones with current technology. This is because, while human brains are able to quickly understand traffic cones, temporary signs, and hand signals from a worker, current AI cannot. These things vary from zone to zone, and AI quickly becomes confused. Human drivers must take the wheel. Despite this, autonomous car companies have been pushing for laws that will allow self-driving vehicles to operate soon.

Those efforts faced a big setback on March 19, 2018. An Uber vehicle hit and killed a pedestrian. There was a human operator, but the vehicle was in self-driving mode. This was the first death involving a self-driving vehicle. Uber suspended all testing of self-driving vehicles in North America and looked into the accident. This event only further worried the many people who fear that AI is not intelligent enough to handle all of the situations that arise on the road. Experts said the accident would delay progress in speeding up laws that allow self-driving vehicle sales and use.

DANGERS OF AI

Renowned scientist Stephen Hawking was among several AI experts who have warned of the potential difficulties posed by AI. During a 2017 technology conference, Hawking stated,

> unless we learn how to prepare for, and avoid, the potential risks, AI could be the worst event in the history of our civilization. It brings dangers, like powerful autonomous weapons, or new ways for the few to oppress the many. It could bring great disruption to our economy.[30]

Scientists and governments around the world are working together to prevent these possible threats. European legislators have proposed restrictions and guidelines surrounding AI development. In 2016,

Stephen Hawking was a famous astrophysicist who warned of the dangers of AI to society. He died in 2018 at the age of 76.

the US National Science and Technology Council recommended monitoring the safety and fairness of developing AI technologies while strengthening the workforce.

In 2015, the Future of Life Institute released an open letter on autonomous weapons. The letter asked governments of the world to resist the temptation to begin an AI arms race. The letter compared a ban on AI arms with international bans on the use of chemical weapons. Its final recommendation was for "a ban on offensive autonomous weapons beyond meaningful human control."[31] Thousands of robotic and AI researchers and scientists signed the letter, including Stephen Hawking, Apple cofounder Steve

Wozniak, and **cognitive** scientist Noam Chomsky.

Human rights groups such as the International Committee of the Red Cross and Human Rights Watch have made similar recommendations. In 2013, the United Nations (UN) formed a group of experts to study the military and ethical aspects of what it called Lethal Autonomous Weapons Systems. Many members of the UN have called for an outright ban on autonomous weapons. However, the UN has yet to make any final recommendations.

Will these measures be enough to protect society from the pitfalls of artificial intelligence? Hawking remained optimistic despite the concerns. "I believe that we can create AI for the good of the world," Hawking said. "That it can work in harmony with us. We simply need to be aware of the dangers, identify them, employ the best possible practice and management, and prepare for its consequences well in advance."[32]

LEARNING FROM THE PAST

Max Tegmark is a physics professor and president of the Future of Life Institute. Tegmark examines how humans have adjusted to new technologies in the past. He uses fire as an example. Thousands of years ago, fire brought mankind into a new era of civilization, Tegmark says. It also brought about house fires, wildfires, and serious burn trauma. Humans reacted by developing fire alarms, smoke detectors, and fire services to prevent future disasters and accidents. Just as with these past technologies, Tegmark says, society must manage the risks of artificial intelligence so that they don't outweigh the benefits. However, losing control of AI weapons and machines could be globally catastrophic. So, Tegmark says, trial-and-error learning no longer serves society well. "We should become more proactive than reactive," says Tegmark, "investing in safety research aimed at preventing accidents from happening even once. This is why society invests more in nuclear-reactor safety than mousetrap safety."[33]

Many AI experts have turned their attention to preventing AI catastrophes. Experts predict two likely scenarios for how much AI could go awry. First, AI technology, such as autonomous weapons, could be programmed to harm humans. In the hands of a dictator or terrorist, these weapons could create mass casualties. If other governments race to develop AI weapons to protect themselves, the technology and its use could quickly spiral out of control.

Second—and perhaps even more alarming—is the risk of beneficial AI that develops a destructive method for achieving a positive goal. For example, a person might ask an autonomous car to drive to a destination quickly. The car might speed, breaking the law to do so. This could occur if the AI's values are not in line with those of humans. Teaching a machine to make decisions like a human can be strikingly difficult. A machine may achieve its goals in the most efficient manner without considering important repercussions. Repercussions could be catastrophic to the economy, the environment, or even fragile diplomatic agreements between nations. To prevent either scenario, experts recommend placing strong controls on AI from the start.

Nick Bostrom is a philosopher who focuses on AI risks. Bostrom outlines a number of methods for preventing destructive AI. Setting limits on future AGI is necessary for human survival. Bostrom says that capability control methods can be used to limit what AI can accomplish. For example, developers can box in a system by blocking its internet access. The machine could also be placed in a Faraday

Faraday Cages use a metal mesh to control electricity. They can be used to block lightning.

cage, an enclosure that physically blocks the machine from sending out radio signals. Developers could offer the AI system incentives to behave in an appropriate manner. Stunting is another effective capability control method in which an AI program is limited by hardware that is slow or short on memory. Lastly, developers could install a mechanism with tripwires in a program. The mechanism scans the system without its knowledge and shuts down the AI if it shows signs of dangerous behavior.

Motivational selection methods could also be used to prevent harmful effects of AI. Shaping the AI's motivations prevents undesirable outcomes. One method of motivational selection is called direct specification. In direct specification, programmers explicitly state a set of rules that the AI program must follow. One example is the Three Laws of Robotics, created by science-fiction author Isaac Asimov.

ASIMOV'S THREE RULES OF ROBOTICS

In 1942, Asimov's short story "Runaround" outlined three rules that robots had to obey. First, a robot cannot hurt a person or let a person be hurt. Second, a robot needs to follow people's orders except if those orders violate the first rule. Third, a robot should protect itself as long as that does not violate the first or second rules.

Asimov later expanded protection to all of humanity with a law zero: "A robot may not harm humanity, or, by inaction, allow humanity to come to harm."[34] The three rules are part of a fictional work. Asimov believed, however, that they could be used to determine the behavior of intelligent machines. Today, Asimov's rules of robotics are still discussed. However, they've been dismissed as a serious tool for managing AI machines with superhuman intelligence.

AI experts today maintain that Asimov's rules are too vague and based on an outmoded idea of ethics. They also point out that Asimov's rules were designed to fail in ways that made for interesting fiction but disastrous reality. So, if AI won't follow the rules, what's the best way to ensure human-friendly AI? In short, says Tegmark, we don't yet know.

"Perhaps there's a way of designing a self-improving AI that's guaranteed to retain human-friendly goals forever," Tegmark says, "but I think it's fair to say that we don't yet know how to build one—or even whether it's possible. . . . It's safest to start devoting our best efforts to them now, long before any superintelligence is developed, to ensure that we'll have the answers when we need them."[35]

What Is the Future of AI?

Many experts are optimistic about the future of AI. They believe that artificial intelligence will benefit society, from shortening workdays to addressing **climate change**. However, they also recognize the challenges AI presents to society and the challenges researchers face in advancing the field. While weak AI has proven useful, AGI remains out of reach.

TEACHING COMMON SENSE

One of the obstacles to developing AGI is the lack of common sense in machines. Rodney Brooks believes that the lack of common sense is a major obstacle to AGI. "Modern day AGI research . . . seems stuck on the same issues in reasoning and common sense that AI has had problems with for at least fifty years," says Brooks.[36]

To better understand the difficulty that common sense presents to AI, consider the sentence, "John left the room." Humans, who live in the same world as John, envision a man walking through a doorway. To humans, this knowledge is considered common sense. An AI program, however, might conceive of John being in a room and then out of it. The program would have no understanding of a door without being told there was a door. Humans develop common sense by interacting with their environment in a way that computers cannot. So developers have to teach AI about how the world works. "Teaching common sense to machines is a major obstacle to progress in AI," agrees Yann LeCun. LeCun adds that most of today's AI only understands "what we feed them through supervised learning."[37] But supervised learning would be impractical for AGI. For an AI machine to develop human-level common sense would require a prohibitive amount of labeling and human oversight. So scientists are hoping to use unsupervised learning more in the future. Because unsupervised learning reduces a machine's reliance on humans, experts say this may make it key to developing AGI with human-like common sense.

COMPUTING POWER

Another barrier to AGI is the current limitations in computing power. Researchers today are looking for ways to increase this power, perhaps by using **quantum** computing. Quantum computing builds on quantum theory, which describes the behavior of subatomic particles. In classical computing, a bit of information can exist in only one of two states—1 or 0. Quantum computing uses quantum bits, called qubits, which can hold multiple values. As a result, calculations can be made more quickly and efficiently. AI experts hope that the development of technologies like quantum computers in the near future will help make AGI a reality.

Deep learning methods have produced agile weak AI. Can technology build on deep learning methods to build AGI? Experts say that isn't likely, due to the amount of data AGI would require. While a young human can learn to recognize a cat with only a few examples, deep learning machines require millions of examples. Also, deep learning techniques aren't perfect. An AI

> **WORDS IN CONTEXT**
>
> **climate change**
> The overall change in global or regional climate patterns; also called global warming.
>
> **quantum**
> Having to do with the nature and behavior of matter at the subatomic level.

machine could easily mistake the image of a cat for a mouse. Those kinds of mistakes might be humorous with weak AI, like that found in image recognition software. However, if an AGI machine tasked with pest control makes such a mistake, the results could be more serious.

When will AI with human-level intelligence be available? Not any time soon, experts say. According to a 2016 White House report on AI, "there is a long history of excessive optimism about AI. . . . It is tempting but incorrect to . . . overlook the huge gap between narrow task-oriented performance and the type of general intelligence that people exhibit."[38] Advancements will take time. Expert opinions vary on when human-level intelligence will be available in machines, but most agree that today's AI technology will eventually lead to AGI.

No one knows if AI developers will be able to overcome hurdles like common sense, nor do they know when AGI will be a reality. But they have a pretty good idea of what the AGI of the future will look like. AGI technology will have memories of past experiences that will help it solve completely new problems. It might be so intelligent that it could seem human, thereby passing the Imitation Game. Apple cofounder Steve Wozniak says that AGI will be able to go into the average American home and make a great cup of coffee. Other AI experts expect AGI to hold down a job, enroll in university, and have a meaningful conversation with a human. Anything humans can do, AGI will be able to do as well.

THE INTERNET OF THINGS

A possible result of AI technology is growth in the Internet of Things (IoT). The Internet of Things is a network of devices that are connected by the internet. Smart thermostats, for instance, allow homeowners to monitor the temperature throughout their houses remotely. They can turn the thermostats up or down. Thermostats and other smart

People enjoy the convenience of devices such as Amazon Echo. Users can listen to music or change the house temperature with a verbal command.

household appliances can connect to smart assistants like the Amazon Echo and smartphones. This connection allows homeowners to control these devices from anywhere.

The number of smart homes will grow in the future. Experts predict there will be approximately 300 million smart home users around the world by 2020. By 2021, homeowners will be spending $1.4 trillion on IoT devices. By 2025, IoT technology will contribute up to $11 trillion to the global economy.

This increase is fueled by improving technology and decreasing cost to consumers. Smart home technology will be better quality and more user friendly, thanks to advances in AI technology such as natural language processing. It will be easier for homeowners to lock or unlock their doors remotely, order groceries from their refrigerators, and even feed their pets with an app. Smart assistants will also help family members check in on elderly relatives from miles away. Meanwhile, the technology will become more affordable for the average consumer.

Concerns about personal privacy and the hacking of connected devices persist, and they will need to be addressed. However, experts say the benefits of the IoT will outweigh the risks. IoT will help people stay connected to their homes, their loved ones, and their communities. IoT technology will add to the global economy. Some experts believe it may even help the environment and decrease or slow climate change. "If you can manage energy better and increase energy efficiency, you can . . . perhaps hold off global warming or at least slow it down,"[39] says John Barrett, a professor at Cork Institute of Technology in Ireland. Smart devices in homes and office buildings are already helping users monitor and reduce their energy usage.

Similarly to smart homes, autonomous cars continue to grow in popularity. Many companies would like to see not just robotaxis but fully automated vehicles in every driveway. Ford, Tesla, GE, Apple, Uber, and Google are all racing to create Level 5 vehicles for the public. What will a society with fully autonomous robotaxis and vehicles look like? Experts say that soon cars may resemble offices or hotels on wheels. They may have comfy sofas and chairs. Travelers will order a vehicle, which will arrive on time and whisk them off to their destination. While en route, passengers will eat, sleep, or even continue working. Fully autonomous AI taxis will give passengers more free time and remove the need for large parking lots in cities. Even more importantly, autonomous vehicles could reduce congestion and virtually eliminate accidents, all thanks to advanced technology based on AI.

AI AND ROBOTICS

No discussion about the future of artificial intelligence would be complete without robotics. The two fields have become synonymous, thanks to science fiction movies and books. Developers are still many years from creating autonomous robots. However, the number of smart machines and robots used in homes will grow over the next fifteen years, according to a 2016 study conducted by Stanford University. The study suggests that AI robots will become more complex and soon "deliver packages, clean offices, and enhance security."[40] Robots will also be more accessible, thanks to research funding by large corporations such as Amazon Robotics, the decreasing cost of manufacturing parts such as 3D sensors, and advances in technology.

Smart robots will benefit many people, but the elderly especially have much to gain, says Cynthia Matuszek. Matuszek is an assistant professor of computer science and **electrical engineering** at the University of Maryland. Matuszek says that AI robots could help elderly people remain independent at home. "I believe artificial intelligence has the potential not only to care for our elders but to do so in a way that

WORDS IN CONTEXT

electrical engineering
The use of science and math to make electricity helpful for people.

increases their independence and reduces their social isolation," says Matuszek. Matuszek points out that robots are especially suited to caring for the elderly because they can work around-the-clock without rest. She also adds that, "since using devices isn't the same as asking someone for help, relying on caregiving robots may lead seniors to perceive less lost autonomy than when they depend on human helpers."[41]

AI robots are also being developed that will lift patients in and out of bed, dispense medicines, monitor patients, and assist with tasks like drawing blood and checking **vital signs**. These robots will free up human caregivers to better meet patients' needs. They may also be able to demonstrate empathy and other emotions generally associated with human caregivers.

As helpful as these smart machines may be, maintaining multiple robots can be expensive and a lot of work. One day, a single, autonomous unit may replace these many smaller robots. These autonomous robots of the future will build on current technologies. They will mimic emotions like Pepper. They will navigate a room autonomously like a Roomba vacuum. They will respond to voice commands like Amazon Echo. Experts warn, however, that people could come to rely too heavily on these machines, and they may eventually take people's jobs.

THE ECONOMY

If AI technologies replace humans across diverse fields, experts wonder how it will impact the economy. If robots can replace even experienced, trained surgeons, how will humans be able to compete? Which careers will no longer be available? Who will benefit the most from AI, and who has the most to lose?

Erik Brynjolfsson of the MIT Sloan School of Management studies how technology and the economy interact. He believes AI will be very helpful to society, but will also present difficulties: "Technological progress is going to leave behind some people, perhaps even a lot of people, as it races ahead." [42] Brynjolfsson states that workers with ordinary skills that can be replaced with automation are most at risk.

In 2017, professional services network PricewaterhouseCoopers published a report discussing how AI and other technologies will change the workforce in the future. The report indicates that employers will value workers with soft skills not yet mastered by AI. These soft skills include leadership, emotional intelligence, empathy, innovation, and creativity. These skills were rated even higher than skills related to science, technology, engineering, and math.

By far, the most valuable skill employees can develop, however, is adaptability. AI affects a wide array of fields and the technology is changing rapidly. Experts find it difficult to predict the next five years, much less the next twenty. So future workers need to be willing to adapt to changing markets. They need to be able to retrain in midcareer and remain open to new experiences and technologies. For flexible workers open to a lifetime of learning, the future is bright.

AI is also producing an effect called "creative destruction," according to Dr. Andrew Chamberlain of Glassdoor Economic Research. Glassdoor conducts research on the labor market. Chamberlain says that although AI is disrupting and destroying many existing jobs, it's also creating new roles in unexpected places. Developing roles include AI journalists and marketing copywriters, technical sales persons, and business developers. In the end, says Chamberlain, "technological advances almost always end up creating more jobs than they destroy."[43] These advances will drive up US productivity and living standards.

Experts say that AI will have other impacts on the modern workforce, including shortening the average workweek. Just as past farm workers left twelve-hour days in the fields for eight-hour workdays in the city, future employees could have AI to thank for shorter hours. This would leave more free time for pursuing hobbies and recreation. K.R. Sanjiv, chief technology officer of Wipro Ltd., an IT services firm, envisions a world with AI. He says:

> We will have a three-day work week because machines would take care of the transactional activities that take up a large chunk of our working hours. This will give us more time to meditate on problems of a much higher order, meet friends, go out with the family, watch movies, read books and, of course, pack our bags to go off to Kotor or Outer Mongolia to expand human consciousness.[44]

Artificial intelligence technology could raise the standard of living and free people from dull tasks to focus more on personal fulfillment. However, technology is changing so quickly that many people could be left behind. If only a few benefit unfairly from AI, then society risks civil unrest and instability. Many cultures are considering innovative ways to share the economic advantages.

ECONOMIC FAIRNESS IN THE AGE OF AI

One controversial solution to this inequity is universal basic income (UBI). UBI would provide a safety net of monthly income to people of eligible working age. Unlike unemployment benefits, the payments would not stop if a person got a job. Proponents say that UBI incentivizes people to find work, rather than punishing them by taking away benefits.

In 2017, Finland began testing UBI with 2,000 unemployed citizens. Citizens were given 560 euros, approximately $670, every month for two years. Participants did not have to report on how they spent the money or whether or not they were looking for jobs. After five months, participants reported less stress, greater incentive to find work, and more free time to pursue **entrepreneurial** ideas. Though the program is expensive, experts believe it will lower other costs to society associated with mental health issues and poverty.

Supporters of universal basic income include many prominent entrepreneurs, including investment company Virgin founder Sir Richard Branson. Branson views a combination of job creation and basic income as key to providing fair treatment. Branson said in an interview with *Business Insider*:

> **WORDS IN CONTEXT**
> **entrepreneurial**
> Having to do with someone who starts a business.

If a lot more wealth is created by AI, the least that the country should be able to do is that a lot of that wealth that is created by AI goes back into making sure that everybody has a safety net. Obviously AI is a challenge to the world in that there's a possibility that it will take a lot of jobs away. . . . It's up to all of us to be entrepreneurially minded enough to create those new jobs.[45]

Not everyone is as optimistic about UBI. Former US vice president Joe Biden believes that work is a basic human necessity that provides individuals with a sense of community, purpose, and dignity. Brynjolfsson agrees with Biden. "It's tremendously important for people to work not just because that's how they get their money, but also because it's one of the principal ways they get many other important things: self-worth, community, engagement, healthy values, structure, and dignity." [46] Though there's no one clear solution, it is widely accepted that AI will impact jobs in the near future. Society will need to find ways to help people adapt to a constantly changing environment. This is especially true as, one day, society may find that these artificial intelligence machines are too smart for their own good.

SUPERINTELLIGENCE

Many AI experts warn that once machines gain general intelligence, they will quickly become superintelligent. They will improve on themselves until they can outsmart and manipulate humans. Machines could demonstrate superintelligence in a number of ways, according to Nick Bostrom. Speed superintelligence would be able to do everything a human can do, only much faster. "An emulation operating at a speed of ten thousand times that of a biological brain," says Bostrom, "would be able to read a book in a few seconds and write a PhD thesis in an afternoon." [47]

The second form is collective superintelligence. This would occur if a network of machines pooled their intelligence, working together as humans do. Experts imagine an Internet of Things no longer interested in doing humans' bidding. The result of machine collaboration would be more advanced than if it had human input.

Third, quality superintelligence would work at least as fast as a human mind while being able to make smarter decisions or have better strategy. The results of any kind of AI superintelligence, according to Bostrom, are equal. Superintelligent machines could quickly become the dominant intelligent life form on planet Earth.

THE FIRST CHURCH OF AI

In 2015, Anthony Levandowski founded the Way of the Future church in California. It isn't a typical church. Instead, future members of the church will focus on the worship of superintelligent AI. Levandowski is an unlikely religious leader. The former Google and Waymo driverless-car developer is most famous for being sued. He was accused of stealing thousands of pages of confidential materials and handing them over to Uber. Levandowski says, however, that a church devoted to AI is a serious and honest endeavor. "What is going to be created will effectively be a god," Levandowski says. "If there is something a billion times smarter than the smartest human, what else are you going to call it?"

The church's members will fund research into creating superintelligent AI. The church will also conduct workshops and educational programs. Levandowski says that superintelligent machines are inevitable and that they will eventually be in charge of Earth. He and his followers want to make sure that intelligent machines know who helped bring them into existence. The church also wants to smooth the transition from human to machine power should that day come. "I would love for the machines to see us as its beloved elders that it respects and takes care of," says Levandowski.

Mark Harris, "Inside the First Church of Artificial Intelligence," *Wired*, November 15, 2017. wired.com.

THE SINGULARITY

Superintelligent AI machines would be able to improve on their own design many times over. They might even create other machines to do their bidding, much as humans created them. Experts call this explosion in intelligence technology the singularity.

The technological singularity is a theoretical phenomenon first described by mathematician I.J. Good in 1965. Good proposed that once AGI machines are created, they will improve upon themselves faster than nature, physics, or certainly society could adapt.

"An ultraintelligent machine could design even better machines," Good claimed in a 1965 paper. "There would then unquestionably be an 'intelligence explosion,' and the intelligence of man would be left far behind. Thus the first ultraintelligent machine is the last invention that man need ever make." [48]

The AI community is split on whether or not researchers should be worried about superintelligent machines. Some AI experts say that superintelligent AI belongs to science fiction and distracts from the very real work being done in AI today. Other experts believe that the risks of developing an intelligent life form should be considered carefully.

Renowned AI expert Stuart Russell describes the two sides of the argument: "We don't worry about remote but species-ending possibilities such as black holes materializing in near-Earth orbit, so why worry about superintelligent AI? Answer: if physicists were working to make such black holes, wouldn't we ask them if it was safe?" [49] Contemporary AI experts including Ray Kurzweil insist that not only is the singularity certain, but that it will occur in the not-so-distant future. Kurzweil is Google's Director of Engineering. He's also known for making accurate predictions about technology. Kurzweil's book *The Singularity Is Near* predicts a singularity will occur by 2045. But he isn't worried about an AI singularity spelling the doom of humanity.

"That's not realistic," Kurzweil said in an interview. "What's actually happening is [machines] are powering all of us. They're making us smarter." [50] Kurzweil and others like him believe that humans will soon merge with smart machines, creating faster, smarter, enhanced humans.

CYBORGS

Elon Musk is working on a new computer-brain **interface**. The futuristic technology merges the latest artificial intelligence with human biology. Also called a neural lace, the technology would be implanted in a brain and allow the brain to interact with a computer. At first, researchers at Musk's company Neuralink will focus on how the technology can relieve the symptoms of chronic disorders affecting the brain, such as epilepsy. Musk hopes that, through AI, technology will eventually enhance human intelligence instead of compete with it.

Machine-enhanced human beings are also called cyborgs. Experts including Musk and Kurzweil believe that cyborg technology will be a positive result of artificial intelligence. For instance, brain-computer interfaces could allow humans to communicate without speaking and control computers with their thoughts. People with amputations can already operate robotic **prostheses** and sense touch through them.

WORDS IN CONTEXT

interface
A technology that allows two systems to interact, such as humans and machines.

prostheses
Artificial body parts generally used by amputees and the disabled.

The enhancements don't have to stop there though. In the future, AI implants could monitor humans' blood pressure or hormone levels. AI prosthetics could make athletes run faster or jump higher. Shimon Whiteson, an AI researcher at the University of Amsterdam, notes, "This has huge implications for basically everything about life."[51] Whiteson imagines people will become more efficient when technology that makes calculations and stores their memories is always with them.

Whiteson admits, however, that cyborg technology will also have its pitfalls. "Society is already wrestling with difficult questions about privacy and security that have been raised by the internet. Imagine when the internet is in your brain, if the US National Security Agency can see into your brain, if hackers can hack into your brain. Imagine if skills could just be downloaded—what's going to happen when we have this kind of AI but only the rich can afford to become cyborgs, what's that going to do to society?"[52] Many experts share Whiteson's concerns. They believe that a discussion about the ethics of AI is an important part of preparing for the future.

AI AND ETHICS

The Partnership for AI to Benefit People and Society was established in 2016. The group's goals include figuring out how AI can be used responsibly, helping people understand AI, and learning how AI impacts the world. Founding partners include corporations like Apple, Facebook, Google, Microsoft, Amazon, and DeepMind. The group gathers insight from industry experts, government officials, nonprofits, and the public on how best to develop socially responsible AI technology. The group hopes that input from diverse backgrounds will reduce the bias already demonstrated by some AI programs.

While groups such as the Partnership are working on solutions, there's still much work to be done. The Royal Society for the Encouragement of Arts, Manufactures and Commerce is a London-based organization that works to find solutions to social problems. In 2017, they recommended that ethics training be a requirement for computer science curriculums. The report also suggests that developers take an oath similar to the Hippocratic Oath

Comic books have imagined a world with cyborgs. DC has featured superhero Victor Stone, called Cyborg, who is part human and part machine.

taken by physicians to do no harm. Since AI is so ubiquitous, its impact is enormous. The issue of AI ethics will require input from all parts of society in order to develop fairly.

THE FUTURE OF ARTIFICIAL INTELLIGENCE AND SOCIETY

Artificial intelligence is a complex and rapidly growing technology. It is also becoming deeply integrated into every facet of society. AI has the potential to make life simpler for everyone and create a more connected, beneficial society.

The risks AI pose are impossible to ignore, though. Artificial intelligence could be used to harm vulnerable populations. The technology may enhance our worst prejudices and fears. It may also turn against us if not properly restrained. However, experts generally believe that the future of AI is bright, so long as all members of society work together to implement AI wisely.

Source Notes

Introduction: Machines That Think

1. Yaniv Taigman, et al., "DeepFace: Closing the Gap to Human-Level Performance in Face Verification," *Facebook Research*, June 24, 2014. research.fb.com.

2. Facebook Research, *Facebook AI Research*, 2018. research.fb.com.

3. Rob Sherman, "Hard Questions: Should I Be Afraid of Face Recognition Technology?" *Newsroom* (blog), *Facebook*, December 19, 2017. research.fb.com.

4. Quoted in Luke Dormehl, "How Facebook's Machines Got So Good at Recognizing Your Face," *Fast Company*, March 29, 2014. www.fastcompany.com.

5. Quoted in Jon Card, "Twilio Chief: 'Machine Learning Has Changed the Game,'" *Telegraph*, August 10, 2017. www.telegraph.co.uk.

6. Quoted in Samuel Gibbs, "Facebook Facing Privacy Actions Across Europe as France Fines Firm €150k," Guardian, May 16, 2017. www.theguardian.com.

Chapter 1: How Does Artificial Intelligence Work?

7. John McCarthy, "What Is Artificial Intelligence? Basic Questions," *Formal Reasoning Group*, November 12, 2007. www-formal.stanford.edu/.

8. McCarthy, "What Is Artificial Intelligence? Basic Questions."

9. Cornell CIS Computer Science, *Unsupervised Learning: The Next Frontier in AI*, 2018. www.cs.cornell.edu.

10. DeepMind, *Research: AlphaGo*, 2018. deepmind.com.

11. Quoted in Will Knight, "AlphaGo Zero Shows Machines Can Become Superhuman Without Any Help," *MIT Technology Review*, October 18, 2017. www.technologyreview.com.

12. Quoted in Kate Baggaley, "There Are Two Kinds of AI, and the Difference Is Important," *Popular Science*, February 23, 2017. www.popsci.com.

13. Quoted in Kristen V. Brown, "Why Artificial Intelligence Always Seems So Far Away," *SF Gate*, January 22, 2015. www.sfgate.com.

14. Quoted in Guia Marie Del Prado, "Experts Explain the Biggest Obstacles to Creating Human-Like Robots," *Business Insider*, March 9, 2016. www.businessinsider.com.

Chapter 2: How Does AI Impact Society?

15. Andrew Ng, "Opening a New Chapter of My Work in AI," *Medium*, March 21, 2017. medium.com.

16. Quoted in Frederic Lardinois, "Andrew Ng's Landing.ai Wants to Bring Artificial Intelligence to the Manufacturing Industry, Starting with Foxconn," *Tech Crunch*, December 14, 2017. techcrunch.com.

17. Quoted in NVIDIA, *NVIDIA Announces World's First AI Computer to Make Robotaxis a Reality*, 2017. nvidianews.nvidia.com.

18. US Centers for Disease Control and Prevention, *Road Traffic Injuries and Deaths—A Global Problem*, November 23, 2016. www.cdc.gov.

19. Max Tegmark, *Life 3.0: Being Human in the Age of Artificial Intelligence*. New York: Alfred A. Knopf, 2017, p. 99.

20. Brian McKenzie. "Who Drives to Work? Commuting by Automobile in the United States: 2013," *United States Census Bureau*, August 13, 2015. census.gov.

21. Quoted in UNC Lineberger, *Pairing Cancer Genomics with Cognitive Computing Highlights Potential Therapeutic Options*, November 20, 2017. unclineberger.org.

22. Quoted in Mike Wehner, "Study Shows Robots Are Better at Slicing Humans Open than Humans Are," *BGR*, October 13, 2017. bgr.com.

23. Homa Alemzadeh, et al., "Adverse Events in Robotic Surgery: A Retrospective Study of 14 Years of FDA Data," *Cornell University Library*, July 21, 2015. arxiv.org.

24. SoftBank Robotics, *Robots: Who Is Pepper?* n.d. www.ald.softbankrobotics.com.

25. Rodney Brooks, "[FoR&AI] Domo Arigato Mr. Roboto," *Rodney Brooks*, August 28, 2017. rodneybrooks.com.

Chapter 3: Can We Trust AI?

26. Julia Angwin, et al., "Machine Bias," *ProPublica*, May 23, 2016. www.propublica.org.

27. Yilun Wang and Michal Kosinksi, "Deep Neural Networks Can Detect Sexual Orientation from Faces," *OSF Home*, 2017, p. 2. osf.io.

28. Quoted in Geoff Spencer, "AI and Cybercrime: Good and Bad News," *Microsoft*, 2018. news.microsoft.com.

29. Quoted in Simson Garfinkel, "Hackers Are the Real Obstacle for Self-Driving Vehicles," *MIT Technology Review*, August 22, 2017. www.technologyreview.com.

30. Quoted in Arjun Kharpal, "Stephen Hawking Says A.I. Could Be 'Worst Event in the History of Our Civilization,'" *CNBC*, November 6, 2017. www.cnbc.com.

31. Future of Life Institute, *Autonomous Weapons: An Open Letter from AI & Robotics Researchers*, July 28, 2015. futureoflife.org.

32. Quoted in Kharpal, "Stephen Hawking Says A.I. Could Be 'Worst Event in the History of Our Civilization.'"

33. Tegmark, *Life 3.0: Being Human in the Age of Artificial Intelligence*, p. 94.

Source Notes Continued

34. "Do We Need Asimov's Laws?" *MIT Technology Review*, May 16, 2014. www.technologyreview.com.

35. Max Tegmark, "Friendly AI: Aligning Goals," Future of Life Institute, August 29, 2017. futureoflife.org.

Chapter 4: What Is the Future of AI?

36. Rodney Brooks, "[FoR&AI] The Seven Deadly Sins of Predicting the Future of AI," *Rodney Brooks*, September 7, 2017. rodneybrooks.com.

37. Yann LeCun, "Obstacles to Progress in AI," *O'Reilly*, September 27, 2016. www.oreilly.com.

38. National Science and Technology Council Committee on Technology, "Preparing for the Future of Artificial Intelligence," *Executive Office of the President of the United States, The White House of President Barack Obama*, October 2016. obamawhitehouse.archives.gov.

39. Quoted in Andrew Weinreich, "The Future of the Smart Home: Smart Homes & IoT: A Century in the Making," *Forbes*, December 18, 2017. www.forbes.com.

40. Peter Stone, et al., "Artificial Intelligence and Life in 2030," *One Hundred Year Study on Artificial Intelligence Report of the 2015–2016 Study Panel*, Stanford University, September 2016, p. 24. ai100.stanford.edu.

42. Erik Brynjolfsson and Andrew McAfee, *The Second Machine Age: Work, Progress, and Prosperity in a Time of Brilliant Technologies*. New York: W. W. Norton & Company, 2014, p. 11.

43. Quoted in Andrew Chamberlain, "Who's Hiring AI Talent in America?" *Glassdoor*, November 16, 2017. www.glassdoor.com.

44. K.R. Sanjiv, "A Three-Day Work Week? It's Possible with Artificial Intelligence," *LiveMint*, December 29, 2017. www.livemint.com.

45. Quoted in Oliver Pechter and Tom Turula, "Richard Branson Discusses Space Travel, AI, and His Friendship with Obama," *Business Insider*, October 9, 2017. www.businessinsider.com.

46. Brynjolfsson and McAfee, *The Second Machine Age: Work, Progress, and Prosperity in a Time of Brilliant Technologies*, p. 234.

47. Nick Bostrom. *Superintelligence: Paths, Dangers, Strategies*. Oxford: Oxford UP, 2014, p. 64.

48. Quoted in George Dvorsky, "Why a Superintelligent Machine May Be the Last Thing We Ever Invent," *Gizmodo*, October 2, 2013. io9.gizmodo.com.

49. Stuart Russell, "Artificial Intelligence: The Future Is Superintelligent," *Nature International Journal of Science*, August 30, 2017. www.nature.com.

50. Quoted in Dom Galeon and Christianna Reedy, "Kurzweil Claims That the Singularity Will Happen by 2045," *Futurism*, October 5, 2017. futurism.com.

51. Quoted in Guia Marie Del Prado, "'We Are All Going to Be Cyborgs' If Humanity Wants to Solve Its Biggest Problems," *Business Insider*, October 15, 2015. www.businessinsider.com.

52. Quoted in Guia Marie Del Prado, "18 Artificial Intelligence Researchers Reveal the Profound Changes Coming to Our Lives," *Business Insider*, October 26, 2015. www.businessinsider.com.

For Further Research

Books

John Allen, *What Is the Future of Artificial Intelligence?* San Diego: ReferencePoint, 2017.

Racquel Foran, *Robotics: From Automatons to the Roomba*. Minneapolis, MN: Abdo, 2015.

Kathryn Hulick, *Artificial Intelligence*. Minneapolis, MN: Abdo, 2016.

Stephanie Sammartino McPherson, *Artificial Intelligence: Building Smarter Machines*. Minneapolis, MN: Twenty-First Century, 2018.

Don Nardo, *How Robotics Is Changing Society*. San Diego: ReferencePoint, 2016.

Internet Sources

Alex Campolo, Madelyn Sanfillippo, Meredith Whittaker, and Kate Crawford, "AI Now 2017 Report," *AI Now Institute*, 2017. ainowinstitute.org.

National Science and Technology Council Committee on Technology, "Artificial Intelligence, Automation, and the Economy," *Executive Office of the President of the United States, The White House of President Barack Obama*, December 2016. obamawhitehouse.archives.gov.

National Science and Technology Council Committee on Technology, "Preparing for the Future of Artificial Intelligence," *Executive Office of the President of the United States, The White House of President Barack Obama*, October 2016. obamawhitehouse.archives.gov.

Websites

Experiments with Google: AI Experiments

experiments.withgoogle.com/ai

This website features a collection of experiments using AI and designed to encourage individual experimentation.

Future of Life Institute

futureoflife.org

Learn more about the Future of Life Institute, founded by author and scientist Max Tegmark. Find a library of the latest research and opinions on developing beneficial AI.

MIT News: Topic Artificial Intelligence

http://news.mit.edu/topic/artificial-intelligence2

A source for news on the latest AI developments. Compiled by the Massachusetts Institute of Technology (MIT).

NASA: Artificial Intelligence Group of the Jet Propulsion Laboratory

https://ai.jpl.nasa.gov/

The site of NASA's AI group in the Jet Propulsion Laboratory. Explore the latest news about AI technology being used in space exploration.

UC Berkeley: Center for Human-Compatible AI

http://humancompatible.ai/

This website is the home of the Center for Human-Compatible AI. Read articles and videos on cutting-edge AI by leading practitioners like Stuart Russell and Andrew Ng.

Index

76

About the Author

Christa C. Hogan is the author of books and articles for kids, teens, and adults. She also parents three avid technology users and is married to a software developer.